T0356932

A Path

TO THE

World

Also by Lori Marie Carlson-Hijuelos

Edited Anthologies

Where Angels Glide at Dawn (co-edited with Cynthia Ventura)
Cool Salsa
Barrio Streets, Carnival Dreams
American Eyes
Moccasin Thunder
You're On!
Red Hot Salsa
Burnt Sugar: Caña Quemada (co-edited with Oscar Hijuelos)
Voices in First Person

Picture Books

Sol a Sol
Hurray for Three Kings Day!

Novels

The Sunday Tertulia
The Flamboyant
A Stitch in Air

A Path TO THE World

Becoming You

Edited by Lori Marie Carlson-Hijuelos

A Caitlyn Dlouhy Book

𝒜 New York London Toronto Sydney New Delhi
atheneum

atheneum

An imprint of Simon & Schuster Children's Publishing Division
1230 Avenue of the Americas, New York, New York 10020
Compilation © 2022 by Lori Marie Carlson-Hijuelos
Pages 101–106 function as an extension of the copyright page.
Jacket design by Karyn Lee © 2022 by Simon & Schuster, Inc.
All rights reserved, including the right of reproduction in whole or in part in any form.
Atheneum logo is a trademark of Simon & Schuster, Inc.
For information about special discounts for bulk purchases, please contact
Simon & Schuster Special Sales at 1-866-506-1949 or business@simonandschuster.com.
The Simon & Schuster Speakers Bureau can bring authors to your live event.
For more information or to book an event, contact the Simon & Schuster Speakers Bureau at
1-866-248-3049 or visit our website at www.simonspeakers.com.
Interior design by Karyn Lee
The text for this book was set in New Caledonia LT Std.
The illustrations for this book were rendered digitally.
Jacket manufactured in China, interior and case manufactured in the United States of America
First Edition
10 9 8 7 6 5 4 3 2 1
Library of Congress Cataloging-in-Publication Data
Names: Carlson, Lori M., editor.
Title: Path to the world : becoming you / [edited by] Lori Carlson-Hijuelos.
Description: First edition. | New York : Atheneum, [2022] | "A Caitlyn Dlouhy book." |
Audience: Ages 14 and up | Audience: Grades 10–12 | Summary: "A chorus of essays from a
variety of voices, backgrounds, and experiences, exploring what it means to be human and true
to yourself. What does it mean to be yourself? To be born here or somewhere else? To be from
one family instead of another? What does it mean to be human? Collected by Lori Carlson-
Hijuelos, A Path to the World showcases essays by a vast variety of luminaries—from Gary Soto
to Nawal Nasrallah to Ying Ying Yu, from chefs to artists to teens to philosophers to politicians
(keep your eyes peeled for a surprise appearance by George Washington)—all of which speak to
the common thread of humanity, the desire to be your truest self, and to belong"— Provided by
publisher.
Identifiers: LCCN 2021021988 | ISBN 9781481419758 (hardcover) | ISBN 9781481419772
(paperback) | ISBN 9781481419796 (ebook)
Subjects: LCSH: Youth—Conduct of life. | Self. | Identity (Psychology) | Belonging (Social
psychology)
Classification: LCC BJ1661 .P29 2022 | DDC 155.5/3—dc23/eng/20211004
LC record available at https://lccn.loc.gov/2021021988

In loving memory of Oscar Hijuelos, my husband,
and my father Robert V. Carlson

Editor's Note

Imagine making an important decision. You might write down on paper the pros and cons of going one way or the other, read the positives and negatives again and again and finally come to a simple conclusion: no matter the choice . . . your life is never going to be the same. This you know for sure. But the tricky part? You can't tell if the outcome will be for better or worse. The uncertainty nags.

Who do you ask for advice? Who can help you make the right choice? A solid decision, after all, is made after considering multiple views and opinions along with having as much applicable information to the issue at hand as possible.

The writers whose ruminations and reflections—about civics, ethics, history, art, and culture—that I have sought to present in *A Path to the World* have had such moments because anyone who commits to what he/she is meant to become fully has to make difficult choices along life's way.

It is hard to be human. It is challenging on several levels—emotional, mental, physical—every single day. And it is daunting to be on the cusp of adulthood; no doubt about it.

But the good news is this: no matter the choices you make in life, the results can be shaped by your attitude. You have the ability—the dynamism and spirit within your being—to decide how to respond to any context in which you find yourself. Even during the times when your prospects seem bleak. Maybe especially so.

As you venture forward on your unique, individual path, you will learn not only through formal education but also through experience. The events that determine the north, south, east, and west of your journey are not determinate; they are winds that come and go. They give your existence its particular slant, yes. But you are the only person who owns the truth of your life as you perceive it . . . not as others see it. That's called treasure.

This collection is eclectic in content, style, and tone. Some ruminations are funny and straightforward while others are philosophical, even didactic. Pat Conroy, for instance, shares his gotta-have recipe for mayonnaise. Otherwise, how can you make a perfect turkey sandwich? Ying Ying Yu explains that being dutiful is more important to her than seeking personal pleasure in order to truly honor her family. Is it any wonder that our country's first president, George Washington, affirms the essence and foundational truth of religious freedom in our land? And in this age of cosmetic obsession, Joseph Bruchac counters the trope of what is acceptably "good looking."

I hope that having read this anthology of opinions, provocations, and conundrums whether front to back, back to front, or in the middle and every which way, you think of the writers in this book as newfound friends who—like friends do—surprise you, assure you, challenge and inspire you on the way to becoming the person you were born to be.

Contents

A Path

TO THE

World

From **Notes of a Translator's Son**

by Joseph Bruchac

My name is Joseph Bruchac. The given name is that of a Christian saint—in the best Catholic tradition. The surname is from my father's people. It was shortened from Bruchacek—"big belly" in Slovak. Yet my identity has been affected less by middle European ancestry and Christian teachings (good as they are in their seldom-seen practice) than by that small part of my blood which is American Indian and which comes to me from a grandfather who raised me and a mother who was almost a stranger to me. I have other names, as well. One of those names is Quiet Bear. Another, given me by Dewasentah, Clan Mother at Onondaga, is *Gah-neh-go-he-yo*. It means "the Good Mind." There are stories connected to those names, stories for another time.

What do I look like? The features of my face are big: a beaked nose, lips that are too sensitive, and sand-brown eyes and dark eyebrows that lift one at a time like the wings of a bird, a low forehead that looks higher because of receding brown hair, and an Adam's apple like a broken bone, two ears that were normal before wrestling flattened one of them. Unlike my grandfather's, my skin is not brown throughout the seasons but sallow in the winter months, though it tans dark and quickly when the sun's warmth returns. It is, as you might gather, a face I did not used to love.

Today I look at it in the mirror and say, *Bruchac, you're ugly and I like you.*

The face nods back at me and we laugh together.

Cool Beef

by Jeremy Lee

My Ma, ever a considerable talent in the kitchen, served a cold boeuf à la mode for my twenty-first birthday, some years ago. The meal included numerous other delights, but my clearest memory is of the beef, possibly for the pleasing smell that flooded the house as the meat cooked, bringing peace to the usual battlefield of family life. Boeuf à la mode—literally, beef in fashion—is the French equivalent of American pot roast: a joint of beef, traditionally rump roast, simmered with vegetables, wine, brandy, a calf's foot, and herbs until it's tender and richly flavored. It is typically served out of the oven, warm and delicious, the calf's foot having given the juices gorgeous body and substance. But the same dish eats just as well—arguably better—when served cold, in aspic. For this presentation, the meat is cooled, often sliced, and arranged in a mold or terrine, along with carrots or other vegetables. Then the cooking liquid is poured on top and the dish is refrigerated until the juices set—thanks to the gelatin in the calf's foot—into a pure, limpid jelly. For a more elaborate presentation, the meat is put on a platter, covered with partially cooled stock, and garnished with cubed aspic and vegetables.

Slow simmering is one of the oldest and best-loved methods of cooking the less exalted cuts of meat. While boeuf à la mode is usually made from plebeian rump roast, as noted, the illustrious French chef Antonin Carême once offered a recipe for a cold variation made with filet simmered in madeira, brandy, and consommé—and in 1816 he reportedly served the dish, which he dubbed filet de boeuf à la gelée, to the future King George IV of England. Carême's recipe was outrageously indulgent and thus appealed greatly to George, who had a reputation for going one step too far. A filet is a sublime roast, and few would have considered simmering it in madeira. This version is now my favorite—but don't tell my Ma.

From **If You Are What You Eat, Then What Am I?**

by *Geeta Kothari*

Indians eat lentils. I understand this is an absolute, a decree from an unidentifiable authority that watches and judges me.

So what does it mean that I cannot replicate my mother's dal? She and my father show me repeatedly, in their kitchen, in my kitchen. They coach me over the phone, buy me the best cookbooks, and finally write down their secrets. Things I'm supposed to know but don't. Recipes that should be, by now, engraved on my heart.

Living far from the comfort of people who require no explanation for what I do and who I am, I crave the foods we have shared. My mother convinces me that moong is the easiest dal to prepare and yet it fails me every time: bland, watery, a sickly greenish-yellow mush. These imperfect limitations remind me only of what I'm missing.

But I have never been fond of moong dal. At my mother's table it is the last thing I reach for. Now I worry that this antipathy toward dal signals something deeper, that somehow I am not my parents' daughter, not Indian, and because I cannot bear the touch and smell of raw meat, though I can eat it cooked (charred, dry, and over-done), I am not American either.

I worry about a lifetime purgatory in Indian restaurants where I will complain that all the food looks and tastes the same because they've used the same masala.

From **Homemade Mayonnaise**

by Pat Conroy

The invention of the blender and the food processor has turned the making of mayonnaise into a matter of seconds. Here is how to do it: Drop an egg*into your machine. Turn it on. Beat that sucker for five seconds. Have some vegetable or canola oil ready. Pour it in a slow stream through the feed tube. Soon, chemistry happens and magic occurs before your eyes as the egg and oil unite into something glorious. When the mixture is thick, cut the machine off. Add the juice of half a lemon or two shots of red wine vinegar. That's mayonnaise. Add a clove of garlic to it. Turn on the machine until the garlic is blended. That's aioli. Try adding some fresh herbs, and you've got herb mayonnaise. Add one-fourth cup Parmesan cheese and a couple of pinches of cayenne, and you have the fanciest, best-tasting salad dressing you've ever had.

*Editor's note: For safety, use a pasteurized egg.

My Tex Mex Essay

by Jacinto Jesús Cardona

As a Tex Mex, thanks to the Treaty of Guadalupe Hidalgo, I often find myself perplexed standing in front of a convex mirror labeled with the warning: Objects in mirror are closer than they appear.

Tex Mex. Yes, as a Tex Mex I must admit at one time I was in the grip of an inferiority complex. I even went to the flea market to buy me a fake Rolex. No doubt it was my immediate reflex to the word "annex": to append or attach, especially to a larger or more significant thing. But one time, out of the blue, while I was living in a duplex on Woodlawn Avenue, I laughed out loud as I read Lady Macbeth's soliloquy:

"The raven himself is hoarse / That croaks the fatal entrance of Duncan / Under my battlements. Come, you spirits / That tend on mortal thoughts, unsex me here, / And fill me from the crown to the toe-topfull / Of direst cruelty!"

In my own demented way, I had made an "unsex me here" connection between Tex Mex, Mexico, and the United States!

Okay, by now you know I did not know what to write for my Tex Mex Essay, so I decided to just use words that rhyme with Tex Mex and take it from there. I apologize.

If nothing else, I hope you liked the part about the convex mirror. I thought that was cool.

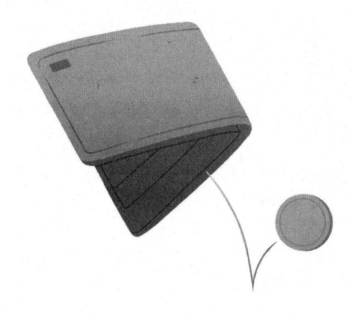

Practicing Medicine Can
Be Grimm Work

by Valerie Gribben

Fairy tales have always fascinated me: fishermen and talking flounder, siblings wending their way through a shadowy forest, seven brothers transformed into ravens. Although I always wanted to be a doctor and took the requisite courses to be admitted to medical school, in my undergraduate years I majored in English and studied Victorian fairy tales. Immersing myself in period documents, I saw tenuous connections between the worlds of fantasy and medicine, between fairy dust and consumption.

But when I started medical school, I packed up my youthful literary indiscretions. I reordered my bookshelf, moving my well-thumbed but now irrelevant Brothers Grimm stories behind a chemistry textbook.

Within weeks my desk was crammed with printouts

on fractures of the humerus and the intermediates of oxidative phosphorylation. I was thinking in terms of proximal and distal, instead of hither and thither.

Then I started my third year of medical school, when students rotate through the different specialties, crisp white coats venturing into the grime of clinical medicine. I felt I was prepared with my color-coded pharmacology flash cards and issues of *The New England Journal of Medicine*.

But soon I came across an elderly woman with hyponatremia, a sodium deficiency. I knew what treatment she needed. But my textbooks and articles let me down. They couldn't tell me why her adult children had been neglecting her and denying her food. They gave no answers to the mysteries behind the physical symptoms, or how to process them.

In pediatrics, my team discovered long, thin scratches on a child's back—made by metal clothes hangers that someone had dug into her skin and pulled.

In physical medicine and rehabilitation, we supervised occupational therapy for a ten-year-old who'd shot himself in the head. He shrugged when we asked why: "I dunno." In neurology, a stroke patient went off life support on his daughter's birthday, and the sound of her convulsive weeping went up and down the hallways, knocking against other patients' doors.

In internal medicine, I cared for a woman who had

been so badly beaten by her late husband that her eyes pointed in different directions. She came in for trouble swallowing, and I had to hold her down during an endoscopy to see if esophageal cancer was the cause.

In surgery, a handsome young man was being eaten alive by cancer.

From above the operating table, I could peer inside him and see tumors wrapping themselves around his vital organs.

In psychiatry, a waifish princess look-alike—mascara dripping down her porcelain cheekbones—was committed to our ward for hearing voices not of this world.

The practice of medicine bestows the sacred privilege to ask about the unmentionable. But what happens when the door to Bluebeard's horror chamber opens, and the bloody secrets spill onto your aseptic field of study? How do you process the pain of your patients?

I found my way back to stories. The Grimm fairy tales once seemed as if they took place in lands far, far away, but I see them now in my everyday hospital rotations. I've met the eternal cast of characters. I've taken down their histories (the abandoned prince, the barren couple) or seen their handiwork (the evil stepmother, the lecherous king).

Fairy tales are, at their core, heightened portrayals of human nature, revealing, as the glare of injury and illness does, the underbelly of mankind. Both fairy tales and medical charts chronicle the bizarre, the unfair, the tragic. And the terrifying things that go bump in the night are what doctors treat at 3 a.m. in emergency rooms.

So I now find comfort in fairy tales. They remind me that happy endings are possible. With a few days of rest and proper medicine, the bewildered princess left relaxed and smiling, with a set of goals and a new job in sight. The endoscopy on my cross-eyed confidante showed she was cancer-free.

They also remind me that what I'm seeing now has come before.

Child endangerment is not an invention of the Facebook age. Elder neglect didn't arrive with Gen X. And discharge summaries are not always happy; "Cinderella" originally ended with a blinding, and Death, in his tattered shroud, waits at the end of many journeys.

Healing, I'm learning, begins with kindness, and most fairy tales teach us to show kindness wherever we can, to the stooped little beggar and the highest nobleman. In another year, I'll be among the new doctors reporting to residency training. And the Brothers Grimm will be with me.

Being Content with Myself

by Kamaal Majeed

"Why don't you act black?"

Since my middle school years, I've been asked this question more than any other. It seems to me that too many people have let society program into their brains what should be expected of me, a black person, before ever interacting with me. But I believe in being who I am, not who others want me to be.

On my first day of high school, going into math class, two of my classmates pointed and laughed at me. I initially thought my fly was open, or that something was stuck in my teeth. But as I took my seat, I heard one of the students whisper, "Why is a black person taking honors?" So my fly wasn't open. An honors-level class had simply been joined by a student whose skin was an unsettling shade of brown.

Many people think my clothes should be big enough

for me to live in, or expect me to listen exclusively to "black music." In seventh grade, a group of my peers fixed their cold stares on my outfit: cargo shorts and a plain, fitting T-shirt. They called out to me, "Go get some 'gangsta' clothes, white boy."

In one of my Spanish classes, as part of a review exercise, the teacher asked me, "¿Te gusta más, la música de rap o rock?" I replied, "La música de rock." The look of shock on my classmates' faces made me feel profoundly alienated.

I am now in my junior year of high school. I still take all honors courses. My wardrobe still consists solely of clothes that are appropriate to my proportions. My music library spans from rock to pop to techno, and almost everything in between. When it comes to choosing my friends, I am still color-blind. I continue to do my best work in school in order to reach my goals; and yet, when I look in the mirror, I still see skin of that same shade of brown.

My skin color has done nothing to change my personality; and my personality has done nothing to change my skin color.

I believe in being myself. I believe that I—not any stereotype—should define who I am and what actions I take in life. In high school, popularity often depends on your willingness to follow trends. And I've been told that it doesn't get much easier going into adulthood. But the only other option is to sacrifice my individuality for the satisfaction and approval of others. Sure, this can be appealing, since choosing to keep my self-respect intact has made me unpopular and disliked at times, with no end to that in sight. But others' being content with me is not nearly as important as my being content with myself.

From **I Came to Duke with an Empty Wallet**

by KellyNoel Waldorf

In my four years at Duke, I have tried to write this article many times. But I was afraid. I was afraid to reveal an integral part of myself. I'm poor.

Why is it not okay for me to talk about such an important part of my identity on Duke's campus? Why is the word "poor" associated with words like "lazy," "unmotivated," and "uneducated"? I am none of those things.

When was the first time I felt uncomfortable at Duke because of money? My second day of o-week. My FAC group wanted to meet at Mad Hatter's Bakery; I went with them and said that I had already eaten on campus because I didn't have cash to spend. Since then, I have continued to notice the presence of overt and subtle class issues and classism on campus. I couldn't find a place for my "poor identity." While writing my resumé, I put McDonald's under work experience. A friend leaned over and said, "Do you think it's a good idea to put that on your resumé?" In her eyes it was better to list no work experience than to list this "lowly" position. I did not understand these mentalities and perceptions of my peers. Yet no one was talking about this discrepancy, this apparent class stratification that I was seeing all around me.

People associate many things with their identity: I'm a woman, I'm queer, I'm a poet. One of the most defining aspects of my identity is being poor. The amount of money (or lack thereof) in my bank account defines almost every decision I make, in a way that being a woman or being queer never has and never will. Not that these are not important as well, just that in my personal experience, they have been less defining. Money influenced the way I grew up and my family dynamics. It continues to influence the schools I choose to go to, the food I eat, the items I buy, and the things I say and do.

I Read Poems Many Times a Day

by Madge McKeithen

I read poems many times a day. I carry them with me in my pocketbook and in my pocket and on my laptop and one in particular on a folded notecard with me always, even at times tucked in my running shoes.

> There is this cave
> In the air behind my body
> That nobody is going to touch:
> A cloister, a silence
> Closing around a blossom of fire.
> When I stand upright in the wind,
> My bones turn to dark emeralds.

James Wright called it "The Jewel"; it is my always poem.

After a day's or a week's or a poet's-worth of reading, I

hold more questions than answers. And better questions. That is the private salvation.

From **Poetry Matters**

by Ralph Fletcher

One year I came home from college to spend Christmas with my family, and I was flat broke. I had gotten used to being a poor college student, but this year I didn't want to be broke for Christmas. I was tired of buying junky gifts for my parents, brothers, and sisters. This year I wanted to have enough money to buy nice presents.

I got a job washing dishes at a local seafood restaurant, stacking trays of dirty dishes and hauling away the clean dishes when they emerged from the dishwashing machine. It was hot, sweaty work, but on Christmas Eve the manager handed me five crisp twenty-dollar bills. I hurried out to do my shopping.

There was a shopping center close to my house. I was walking across the parking lot when I was startled to see my grandfather. He was leaning over a container of trash, picking through it.

"Grandpa?" I said. When I took a step closer I could see that even though the man was tall, thin, and bald he wasn't my grandfather. This ragged man had a ripped coat; he looked cold. All I could imagine was my grandfather pawing through trash, looking for something to eat on Christmas Eve. I walked up to him and pressed the five twenty-dollar bills into his cold hand.

"Merry Christmas," I mumbled.

"Th-thank you, son," the man stammered, looking at the money.

I wanted to tell him to use the money to buy a new coat, but somehow the words wouldn't come out. I turned around and started walking home.

"Merry Christmas!" the man yelled.

"Merry Christmas," I said, waving. When I walked away I felt good.

Turbesi Park

by Emily Lisker

Yesterday in the late afternoon I walked to Turbesi Park.
Lily was frolicking in circles, squeezing an empty plastic
water bottle in her mouth, when she suddenly stopped to
watch a tiny dog in the adjacent ball field with three girls
running after him. The kids were having so much fun, as
if they had entered the outdoors for the first time in their
lives; running, jumping, falling, chasing this fast little
burnt-sienna-colored dog with ears that stood straight
up. Their dad was outside the fence watching them. They
threw a ball and a stick for him to fetch, shouting, "Spud,
fetch!" but he ignored their prompts. He just ran around
in circles.

   After Lily was done running in circles, I put her leash
back on and we walked along the path behind the other
ball field. Spud ran up to the fence and met Lily nose to
nose. Spud was wearing a blue plaid wool sweater. The

girls asked me if I would bring Lily inside to play with them. I said, "I'm worried about Spud getting hurt. He is so delicate."

"What does that mean?" the younger girl asked.

"He has small, fragile arms and legs. Is he a Chihuahua?" I asked.

"No, he's a red miniature Doberman pinscher," the oldest girl said. She had wavy long blond hair and thick black eyelashes. "He's strong and not afraid and runs fast," she said.

"Okay, as long as Lily doesn't knock him over. I wouldn't want him to get hurt. How about if I keep the leash on Lily until they get acquainted?"

"Does your dog chase balls?" the oldest girl asked, handing me a baseball she had found.

"Yes, but she loves empty plastic bottles the best because they are light and she makes them squeak and crunch in her mouth." I threw the empty plastic bottle and Lily ran after it with the red-and-black harlequin-patterned leash trailing on the grass. I ran over and unclipped it. She and Spud circled the field with full energy and joy.

"She runs like a reindeer. Makes me wish I could be a dog and play with a plastic bottle in *my* mouth!" the middle girl said.

The girls laughed and ran after Lily, and the dogs seemed to be laughing too as they ran in high-speed circles and zigzagged around us. The father was amused and stood leaning forward with folded arms, watching and smiling. "Careful, don't get knocked over," I shouted to the girls.

At one point the smallest girl draped her whole body in a shocking pink jacket over Lily, hugging her like a pet pony.

"Our dog doesn't like to chase sticks or balls," the oldest girl said.

"Lily is a Labrador retriever. She's bred to retrieve ducks out of water for hunters. The bottle is like a duck to her; that's why she chases it. I'm sure your dog has special characteristics. Does he dig holes?"

"Yes, sometimes."

"Chase mice?"

"No, we still have plenty of mice."

"Guard your house?"

"Yes!"

"Well, there you go, every dog has special traits. If you look in the encyclopedia, you could probably find the special traits for your kind of dog."

"I heard from someone that the red miniature Dobermans are extra nice," she offered.

The girls didn't want me to leave and I didn't want to leave either. I stayed for a few more rounds of running with the girls and the dogs. Then Lily was tired out and was chewing on grass like a cow and biting at the clay field, which is what she does when she is thirsty and looking for water. I clipped the leash on her and started for the gate. Their dad called the girls to go home for supper. The oldest was carrying Spud like a baby in her arms.

A Duty to Family, Heritage, and Country

by Ying Ying Yu

I am a good child, obedient. I grew up in China, a country where education is the center of every child's life and a grade of less than 85 percent is considered a failure. Grades mean more to us than a mother's smile, more than the murmur of a wish lingering on birthday candles. I had homework during lunch, math and language classes two times a day. There were punishments for not paying attention. I was beaten with a ruler. I learned to do anything to get a good grade.

I believe in duty, but that belief comes with sacrifice. The achievements I make come with a cost.

I remember first grade, the red scarf flapping in the wind, wanting more than anything to be the first one to wear it—the symbol of responsibility, excellence, and loyalty. The first thing that flashed to mind when I put it on was how glad my family would be, how proud the motherland would be of the child it had borne, and how my accomplishments would look on a college application.

All my pride, love, self-esteem, they merge into duty. There have been times I wanted to throw away everything, but duty and obligation were always there to haunt me and to keep me strong. I would think: My parents and grandparents brought me up, my country gave me shelter, my teachers spent so much time building my foundations just to have me throw it all away? No, I can't do that! I must repay all that they have done. "I must," "I should," "I have to," all those little phrases govern my life and the lives of my classmates. We struggle on because duty reminds us that the awaiting success is not just for us. It's for our families, our heritage, and country.

I used to want to be a gardener. I liked working outdoors and the gritty feel of dirt was much more tangible than a bunch of flimsy words strung together. But I can never grow up to be a gardener. Everything I have done so far points to the direction of becoming a lawyer. That's a job my family wholeheartedly supports.

There is no other choice for someone who's been brought up by such a strict system, someone who has ambition. Here in America, there is almost a pressure to follow your dreams. I don't want any more dreams—dreams are illusions. And it's too late for me to work toward another future, to let the foundations I have built go to ruins.

I believe in the power of duty to impel. Only duty will offer me something true, something worthy of my effort and the support of my family and country. Duty can bring me to an achievement that is greater than I am.

Cakes

by Nawal Nasrallah

The Sumerians were conscious of the superiority of their cuisine. Criticizing the way the Bedouins of the western desert had their food, they said if you gave them flour, eggs, and honey for a cake they would not know what to do with them. In addition to such references to cakes, ancient cuneiform tablets going back to the third millennium BC have preserved interesting records with regard to pastry making. We learn that besides the regular breads, they made a better variety by "beating in" various fatty substances, such as vegetable oils and animal fats. Honey was sometimes added. The cakes were made with even higher quality flour and with "noble fat," which might well have been clarified butter. Those cakes took the shape of lumps, rings, crescents, pillars, and even turbans. In the first millennium BC date breads were made by dicing dates and mixing them with oil and flour. They were called "tak-kasu" or "makkasu." There were cuneiform texts that even give proportions in which the ingredients were to be mixed for cakes made to go to the temple and the palace. Evidently, ordinary people did not enjoy such refined cakes. It was beyond their means. Cakes have always been emblematic of luxury, refinement, grace, and beauty. In Iraq today a pretty woman is called *keka*.

Hispanic Heritage

by Raquel Senties

In October, we celebrate Hispanic Heritage month. We celebrate our *raíces*, what we are, what we were, and where we came from. I, personally, as a third-generation American living on the border town of Laredo, Texas, have not experienced the ostracism and hatred that others have. We have always been the majority. Race was just another word in the dictionary. And as the saying goes, we didn't cross the border; the border crossed us. *Gringos* were few and far between. Growing up, the only Black I ever saw as a child was a very old man whose white hair I found amazing. My parents talked about experiencing discrimination in cities beyond Laredo where there were instances of signs on restaurants forbidding entrance to dogs and Mexicans. I didn't experience racism until I attended Texas State College for Women, where a girl asked the teacher why they allowed Mexicans to attend the college when blacks were not.

The history of Hispanics in the United States is the history of the United States itself. The values of the Hispanic community—the love of family, *abuelos*, *primos*, *tíos* who at one time or another have lived with us, a profound and constant faith, and a solid work ethic are the values of the United States. We are endowed with the rich traditions of communities with centuries-old roots in the United States as well as the energy and enterprise of recent immigrants. Many risk their lives to start a new life with the hope of building a better life for themselves and their children.

We are a proud people, proud of our culture, of our family, of our skin color that comes in many shades from white, blue-eyed and blond, to café con leche, wavy brown hair, and hazel eyes, to copper and eyes and hair as dark as a midnight sky. We are proud of our Indian blood as well as our Spanish blood, proud of the Dallas Cowboys and México's El America.

As we continue to enrich the character of our great nation, we bond even closer to the promise of the United States and confirm the American narrative of unity and progress.

Courtesy

by Gary Soto

Dolores Velasco, a former nun and friend of mine at the United Farm Workers, was once invited by a female farm worker to a house built of cardboard. This structure was behind an abandoned barn and away from the road. It was early February, wet, the blossoms from any number of fruit trees blowing across the fields. Dolores couldn't say no and followed this woman, who had been on a picket line for several hours outside of McFarland, California. There, kneeling in the cardboard house, the farm worker took a glass bowl from a box. She peeled three oranges and parted them into wedges, which were then lightly peppered with cayenne and sprinkled with salt. She found a dish towel to serve as a communal napkin. The bowl, a chalice of friendship, was set before them. They ate with their hands, Dolores told me, salt on the edges of her fingers.

What we can learn from such courtesy.

Get Yourself Some Credit

by Shadi Feddin

I am racing down Third Avenue with my college girl-friends in New York City, trying to beat a group of boys—#classic—who want the same apartment as us. We are all recent college graduates, and the group to place the security deposit in the landlord's hand first gets the apartment. We had but five blocks to go when my broker got the call notifying us of our defeat. "Nooooo!" I declared.

"That's okay, that's okay, we'll make them work for us one day!" joked one of my friends in an attempt to lighten the mood. We all stopped walking to bask in our frustration for a minute. The apartment hunt continued the rest of the afternoon, but nothing was as nice and within our budget compared to the one we lost.

The next day, my friends and I received a call from our broker stating that the apartment we loved and had originally lost was available again. "How is that possible?" we all squealed with excitement over the phone. He said, "Two of the boys didn't meet the credit requirement, so it's yours for the taking if you want it." We jumped up and squealed in our victory.

Just four years earlier, my mother had dragged me to a local Wells Fargo branch where my family did its banking to sign up for a college Visa card. She told me it was time to build *credit*, but I didn't care what that meant. It was to be my first official credit card and all I knew was that Visa was the best kind of friend to have when shopping. My mother tried to engage me in the conversation with the banker, urging me to be responsible so as to improve my credit through time. I provided two minutes of head nodding and uh-huhs before proceeding to zone out. As a young woman who got the apartment I wanted right after college graduation, I had a serious moment of deep gratitude toward my mother for helping me build credit early on.

From *What Money Can't Buy:
The Moral Limits of Markets*

by Michael J. Sandel

Why worry that we are moving toward a society in which everything is up for sale?

For two reasons: one is about inequality; the other is about corruption. Consider inequality. In a society where everything is for sale, life is harder for those of modest means. The more money can buy, the more affluence (or the lack of it) matters.

If the only advantage of affluence were the ability to buy yachts, sports cars, and fancy vacations, inequalities of income and wealth would not matter very much. But as money comes to buy more and more—political influence, good medical care, a home in a safe neighborhood rather than a crime-ridden one, access to the elite schools rather than failing ones—the distribution of income and wealth looms larger and larger.

Where all good things are bought and sold, having money makes all the difference in the world.

This explains why the last few decades have been especially hard on poor and middle-class families. Not only has the gap between rich and poor widened, the commodification of everything has sharpened the sting of inequality by making money matter more.

The second reason we should hesitate to put everything up for sale is more difficult to describe. It is not about inequality and fairness but about the corrosive tendency of markets. Putting a price on the good things in life can corrupt them. That's because markets don't only allocate goods; they also express and promote certain attitudes toward the goods being exchanged. Paying kids to read books might get them to read more, but also teach them to regard reading as a chore rather than a source of intrinsic satisfaction. Auctioning seats in the freshman class to the highest bidders might raise revenue but also erode the integrity of the college and the value of its diploma. Hiring mercenaries to fight our wars might spare the lives of our citizens but corrupt the meaning of citizenship.

Economists often assume that markets are inert, that they do not affect the goods they exchange. But this is untrue. Markets leave their mark. Sometimes, market values crowd out nonmarket values worth caring about.

Of course, people disagree about what values are

worth caring about, and why. So to decide what money should—and should not—be able to buy, we have to decide what values should govern the various domains of social and civic life.

Public Good

by William Sloane Coffin

Public good doesn't automatically flow from private virtue. A person's moral character, sterling though it may be, is insufficient to serve the cause of justice, which is to challenge the status quo, to try to make what's legal more moral, to speak truth to power, and to take personal or concerted action against evil, whether in personal or systemic form.

A Parsonage

by Lori Marie Carlson-Hijuelos

For my family and others of the congregation of the Holy Trinity Lutheran Church in southwestern New York, the parsonage seemed just as sacred as the building of the sanctuary, the house of God. The reason was quite simple, really. The pastor and his wife, of Midwestern stock and tradition, were as embracive as the Minnesotan plains and present in the moment: extremely generous hosts. Their brand of hospitality was over the top. The front door on the long, wide porch was always open.

Countless individuals benefited from their kindness: children, young adults, middle-aged and elderly—all could come at any time for words of encouragement, prayers, a few bear hugs. Such gifts came naturally, as surely as golden apples on an autumn tree. Full and abundant; a profusion of warmth. I think the Bergstands likened it to Lutheran hospitality, meaning that a pastor and his spouse, like Martin Luther and his wife, Katharina, so many centuries ago, should grace their home with festive music, flowers, cheer.

Their parsonage, a red-brick and painted clapboard structure, had the look of solid comfort. Inside, the rooms were sunny. Walls the shade of goldenrod, carpeting like wildflowers known as painter's-brush. Burnt-orange. The lawn spread forth as an apron, just to the woods that rolled along the sloping hills in that part of town. And a well-trod path connected the grassy green to the outdoor chapel. Beyond, the pastor's vegetable garden. In the summer, many of the congregants ate delicious melons, squash, and huge cucumbers grown in that garden because the pastor, after church, would pass them out with pride.

Sunday after Sunday, the pastor and his wife opened their entire house, all four bedrooms, kitchen, family room, living room, dining room to the young people, me among them, of the church. In other words, their home was our Sunday school. And it wasn't just the physical space that was made available to us. It was their heart, their laughter. There we would gather, about twenty teens, sitting or kneeling on the floor. In debate. We would discuss important issues of the day and politics, world problems such as poverty and hunger, the deterioration of natural resources, morality, philosophy, world religions. In winter, a roaring fire in the family room would greet us; in spring, huge bouquets of field flowers: daisies, bluebells, forget-me-nots, and buttercups, lots and lots of buttercups. A pot of coffee, a few sweet rolls, and cardamom braids were always on the oval table in the kitchen.

Pastor Bergstrand and his wife and children were our family.

The Octogenarian Cheerleader

by Scott Pitoniak

After retiring in 1988 from the trucking business he had founded, Freddy Schuman began searching for something to occupy all the free time he was about to have on his hands. One day, while scanning the sports pages, the 62-year-old Bronx native was shocked to discover that the mighty Yankees of his youth were in last place and that a cone of silence had enveloped the House That Ruth Built.

"I read where the fans had become apathetic and the stadium was no longer an intimidating place for teams to visit," Schuman recalled. "I wanted to do something to wake Yankee fans up and get them back to supporting their team."

Schuman remembered how his mother used to let him and his siblings bang spoons and pots and pans together on New Year's Eve when the clock struck midnight. He believed if he could walk around the stadium during Yankees games beating a spoon against a frying pan, he'd eventually be able to rouse the spectators from their lethargy.

It sounded like a crazy idea, but then Yankees community relations director Dick Kraft decided to let Schuman give it a try.

"He essentially said, 'You can do it as long as nobody complains,'" Schuman recounted.

No one did.

And the superfan known as Freddy Sez wound up beating not only a frying pan, but the odds.

For the past two decades, the man with the kitchen utensils and the pinstriped Yankees jersey has become a staple at the stadium. The team gives him free admission and free rein, and Schuman takes full advantage of the unlimited access, roaming the upper deck, the loge, and the lower deck during games. Spectators gladly chant, "Let's go, Yankees" with him and often ask him to pose for pictures and sign autographs. Their biggest kick, though, comes when Schuman hands them the spoon, so they can bang away on his battered, metal frying pan.

"My ego gets so pumped up when they do that," he said. "It makes me feel as if I've made a difference."

He said the slang name "Sez" is a takeoff on a name used by a popular New York City dress retailer from a bygone era. Schuman shows up at the park carrying a cardboard sign bearing different slogans.

He's had many thrilling moments as a superfan, but the tops probably was when the Yankees ended an 18-year World Series drought in 1996. The Bronx Bombers rallied from a two-game deficit in that series against the Atlanta Braves to win it all in six. Schuman remembers how the fans at the stadium were reenergized when an eight-year-old boy took hold of the spoon during the final game.

"This kid whacked the devil out of the frying pan, and the fans started making noise, and the Yankees scored three runs and went on to win the game and the series," he said. "It took a little kid to remind people that a ballpark is one of the few places in society where it's all right to make noise."

From **Making Choices**

by Alexandra Stoddard

There are only two kinds of choices available to us. First, the active: we make something happen and live with the consequences. Or we may choose to *not* make a choice; we weigh the facts, decide the price of change is too high, and make the choice to live with things as they are. The second kind of choice, the more dangerous, it seems to me, is the postponement of choice. Procrastination results in apathy, discouragement, and depression. Whenever we turn our backs on what we *know* we need to do, we turn against our higher self. We forego the power to do something positive, to turn the situation around, or open new doors. At times we all want to think about problems tomorrow, but we lose sleep unnecessarily because we forfeit facing the truth. Our inability to confront the heart of the matter causes anxiety. Truth is *always* the right choice.

There is no magic in tomorrow; we can think things through rationally today. There are times, many times, when we just have to look truth in the face, bite the bullet, no matter how nasty or dirty or unpleasant the situation may be, and move on.

An amazing paradox is that it is really easier to be courageous than to be a coward. Once you get over the initial fear of plunging into the unknown, with all its dangers and snake traps, the mere fact that you dared to face a hard decision becomes your ally.

From *The United States of Ambition*

by Alan Ehrenhalt

Who sent these people?

It is not hard to ask that question every now and then during a normal political year, as we find ourselves confronted with officeholders and candidates who fail to meet any commonsense definition of what political leadership ought to be: aspirants for the US Senate who traffic in the basest kind of playground name-calling; governors who win election on anti-tax platforms they know they will have to repudiate; members of Congress who talk endlessly about cutting the federal deficit and never even begin to do it; state legislators who fall for the most heavy-handed bribery schemes cooked up by federal prosecutors to entrap them. Is it possible that this is the best we can do—that this is the best political leadership the world's oldest democracy can muster?

Who sent us the leaders we have? This question forms

itself repeatedly in the recesses of our minds, even as we elect and reelect people who fall pitifully short of our ideals of statesmanship. But oddly enough, we do not pursue the issue very seriously. We love to complain about our politicians even as we return them to office. We debate proposals to limit the number of terms they can serve, in effect seeking a procedural cure for our addiction to reelecting them. What we are reluctant to do is to trace the roots of our discontent.

How did the people who govern us get there in the first place? Why are we being led by this particular set of public officials, and not some other? What sorts of people manage to win election to office these days?

And if, as a group, they continue to disappoint us, term after term, campaign after campaign, is it their fault—or is it ours?

From **George Washington to the Hebrew Congregation in Newport, Rhode Island, 18 August 1790**

by George Washington

To the Hebrew Congregation in Newport, Rhode Island [Newport, R.I., 18 August 1790]

Gentlemen.

While I receive, with much satisfaction, your Address replete with expressions of affection and esteem; I rejoice in the opportunity of assuring you, that I shall always retain a grateful remembrance of the cordial welcome I experienced in my visit to Newport, from all classes of Citizens.

The reflection on the days of difficulty and danger which are past is rendered the more sweet, from a consciousness that they are succeeded by days of uncommon prosperity and security. If we have wisdom to make the best use of the advantages with which we are now favored, we cannot fail, under the just administration of a good Government, to become a great and a happy people.

The Citizens of the United States of America have a right to applaud themselves for having given to mankind examples of an enlarged and liberal policy: a policy worthy of imitation. All possess alike liberty of conscience and immunities of citizenship. It is now no more that toleration is spoken of, as if it was by the indulgence of one class of people, that another enjoyed the exercise of their inherent natural rights. For happily the Government of the United States, which gives to bigotry no sanction, to persecution no assistance, requires only that they who live under its protection should demean themselves as good citizens, in giving it on all occasions their effectual support.

It would be inconsistent with the frankness of my character not to avow that I am pleased with your favorable opinion of my Administration, and fervent wishes for my felicity. May the Children of the Stock of Abraham, who dwell in this land, continue to merit and enjoy the good will of the other Inhabitants; while every one shall sit in safety under his own vine and fig tree, and there shall be none to make him afraid. May the father of all mercies scatter light and not darkness in our paths, and make us all in our several vocations useful here, and in his own due time and way everlastingly happy.

From **Who Let the Dogs In?:**
Incredible Political Animals I Have Known

by Molly Ivins

Did you know that in nineteenth-century America, politics was the entertainment that more than filled in for both television and movies? It was the equivalent of all the college and professional sports teams added together—people listened to politicians giving loooong speeches as though . . . as though their lives depended on it. It was considered better than the zoo, better than the circus, better than the Friday Night Lights. And it wasn't about who won or lost, it was about how your life would turn out. Americans understood that; they knew their decisions mattered.

Where did it go, that understanding? When did politics become about *them—those people* in Washington or *those people* in Austin—instead of about *us*? We own it, we run it; we tell them what to do; it's our country, not theirs. They're just the people we hired to drive the bus for a while. I hear people say, "I'm just not interested in politics." "Oh, they're all crooks anyway." Or *There's nothing I can do."*

Because I have been writing about politics for forty years, I know where the cynicism comes from, and I would not presume to tell you it is misplaced. If the system is so screwed up, if you think it's not worth participating in, then give yourself credit for being alert. But not for being smart. How smart is it to throw away power? How smart is it to throw away the most magnificent political legacy any people has ever received? This is our birthright; we are the heirs; we get it just being born here. "We hold these truths to be self-evident, that all men [and women!] are created equal, that they are endowed by their Creator with certain unalienable Rights, that among these are Life, Liberty and the pursuit of Happiness.—That to secure these rights, Governments are instituted among Men, deriving their just powers from the consent of the governed,—That whenever any Form of Government becomes destructive of these ends, it is the Right of the People to alter or to abolish it." More than two hundred years later, people all over the world are willing to die for a chance to live by those ideals. They died in South Africa, they died at Tiananmen Square, they're dying today in Myanmar.

Don't throw that legacy away out of cynicism or boredom or inanition: "I'm just not interested in *politics*." "There's nothing I can do."

You have more political power than 99 percent of all the people who have ever lived on this planet. You can not only vote, you can register other people to vote, round up your friends, get out and do political education, talk to people, laugh with people, call the radio, write the paper, write your elected representatives, use your e-mail list, put up signs, march, volunteer, and raise hell. All your life, no matter what else you do—butcher, baker, beggarman, thief / doctor, lawyer, Indian chief—you have another job, another responsibility: You are a citizen. It is an obligation that requires attention and effort.

From **Cooperation in Congress? It's in Our Constitutional DNA**

by David E. Skaggs

America's leading idea was and is that we're all created equal. To keep faith with that principle, our representatives need to act out of the mutual respect that equality demands. As elected representatives of constituencies of civic equals, they are obliged to treat one another civilly.

Out of this flows an imperative for civility as a matter of political morality. That is, if compromise is a political and constitutional necessity, and if mutual respect is a moral requirement of our founding principles, then developing politics of civility is essential. This civility stuff is worthy enough in its own right. It makes the business of politics more pleasant.

However, it is also the means needed to reach the goal of bipartisan compromise. That gets us to a human dimension, where psychology, sociology, and politics mix.

We're most likely to feel able to compromise with people we trust.

We're only likely to trust those we've gotten to know. People are not likely to get well acquainted with colleagues who do not treat them decently. We usually look for some minimal show of goodwill from others—especially if they are from another tribe (party).

It follows that civil and respectful behavior among our representatives is essential for them to develop the trust that in turn enables the bipartisan compromises that are needed for contemporary American politics to function.

Being nicer to one another won't get the job done by itself.

Democratic and Republican representatives of goodwill must still do the heavy lifting of working out the compromises needed to solve our problems. But if they choose not to behave well toward one another, progress will almost certainly remain elusive. (And sometimes you wonder whether a certain level of hostility isn't a convenient excuse for avoiding the hard work of compromise.)

From **Reason to Believe**

by Mario Cuomo

With all due respect to the geniuses who first shaped this miracle of a nation, the wisdom of their day was designed to govern a society in which the only people who counted fully as people were landowning, white, Christian men. It is a wisdom we need to govern our own time—but it is not wisdom enough.

As they shaped a new nation, the Founders were exploring the possibilities of a brand-new intellectual prism we now call individualism. It was and is a thing of thrilling power. Pass the American people through that prism and we break up into a magnificent rainbow: 250 million wavelengths unfurled. Seeing it for the first time in history, the Founders thought it was beautiful, and they were right. But we need to remember today that it is only one way of seeing the shaft of light that shines down on this extraordinary place: America is also and equally the bright, warm sunlight in which the colors and differences come together as one. We are also a community—and we must also value that.

Yes, we should remember our past—but remember all of it. We should remember that, in just two hundred years, we invented a society—and saved it from shattering. We defeated the greatest armies mankind ever raised. We have opened our gates and our hearts to ten generations of seekers from every corner of the earth, and made democracy work better than anyone dreamed it could. How? By being honest. Bold. Courageous. And positive. By being better than our worst impulses. And by being more together, than any of us could have been alone. During World War II, throughout the battles for worker protection and public education and Social Security and civil rights, whenever we have been at our very best, we have succeeded, when we might have failed, by recognizing that we have an obligation to one another. Not just because it's a nice idea, but because we need everyone helping to pull the wagon.

We still do. It is a simple truth our hearts already know: we cannot reach the levels of strength and civility we should with one-third of our people striding up the mountain with perfect confidence, one-third desperate in the ditches by the side of the trail, and the third in between wondering whether they'll slip down into the ditch themselves.

Get a Life

by Anna Quindlen

Get a life in which you are generous. Look around at the azaleas making fuchsia star bursts in spring; look at a full moon hanging silver in a black sky on a cold night. And realize that life is glorious, and that you have no business taking it for granted. Care so deeply about its goodness that you want to spread it around. Take the money you would have spent on beers in a bar and give it to charity. Work in a soup kitchen. Tutor a seventh grader.

All of us want to do well. But if we do not do good, too, then doing well will never be enough.

Puzzle Solved, Creatively

by Yuyi Li

Puzzles are mysterious and transparent; each box of puzzles contains an almost infinite set of choices and outcomes, yet the final imagery is almost always constant. When I was in middle school, I spent two weeks of winter holiday sitting on my living room floor . . . transforming a thousand unique puzzle pieces into a cohesive Thomas Kinkade painting. Many years later, I reminisced on that experience and realized, it was then and there that I discovered something about myself and about creativity. For me, creative thinking, the input of creativity, boils down to the puzzle-solving process. It is quite simple—you could rely solely on a calculated and systematic method by grouping similar pieces by attributes such as color, shape, and size. But, at a certain point, there is usually a need to fit pieces together in a random way, ultimately, a test of luck within a system of chaos. Puzzles inspire me to think creatively, to intertwine the status quo with sprinkles of luck within a seemingly chaotic environment; to output, creativity.

I'd Like to Recall Some Times

by Alexandre Hollan

I'd like to recall some times that have led me to this point.

I was born in Hungary, a long time ago, and very early I discovered silence. A large part of my childhood was spent in the countryside, in a property far from everything. At first it seemed boring, but then I sensed a silent and familiar presence in which everything had its own life and shared a common nature with other things. This happy childhood survived, though not easily, through my difficult adolescent years, the political persecutions and my escape from the country in 1956. When I arrived in Paris, my exposure to the contemporary art of the time produced powerful and at times violent questioning, to which I had no answer. I was looking for "something," a little like Rothko or Franz Kline; what they had found filled museums but left me feeling a little empty. I found an answer in 1964 in Paris at a Giorgio Morandi exhibition: yes, what I was looking for was not far.

In those years I continued to move around and search for "a strong and real impression" through travel; I lived in my car and drove thousands of kilometers from Scotland to Tuscany, observing nature and drawing trees.

This wandering ended in the 1980s when I purchased a farmhouse in the south of France. In the ruined house I found two rusty old pots covered in holes and mud. These objects slowly came to life: I would look at them and draw them, and a quiet world appeared. This world of old and used things, whose matter becomes loose, is truly alive. The forms and colors intertwine and guide the gaze into depth. Through this discovery I crossed paths with Morandi again.

Another day, as I was painting a "silent life" for the tenth time, I had the strong sensation that a color had moved, that it had come apart from the whole; it had spilled out of its form and gone everywhere. I myself was immersed in that color, in its light. Now I know that those moments do not last; but I also know they can return. This makes the gaze quieter; and in a quiet gaze, in its space, everything finds a place.

The world awaits our gaze.

An Original Work

by Timothy Egan

An original work, an *aha!* product or a fresh insight is rarely the result of precise calculation at one end producing genius at the other. You need messiness and magic, serendipity and insanity. Creativity comes from time off, and time out.

Contributor Bios

JOSEPH BRUCHAC is an enrolled member of the Nulhegan Band of the Coosuk Abenaki Nation. Founder and executive director of the Greenfield Review Literary Center and the *Greenfield Review Press*, much of his own writing draws on his Native ancestry. He and his grown sons, James and Jesse, also storytellers and writers, work together in projects involving the preservation of Native culture, Native language renewal, and teaching traditional Native skills and environmental education at their Ndakinna Education Center located on their ninety-acre family nature preserve. Bruchac is the author of more than 160 books for young readers and adults. His experience includes three years of volunteer teaching in Ghana, West Africa, and eight years of running a college program in a maximum security prison.

JACINTO JESÚS CARDONA, aka Jesse, is a San Antonio poet, but he grew up in Alice, the Hub of South Texas. His poetry celebrates the *x* in Texas, the *x* in Mex, and the humble *x* his illiterate mother used to make. Cardona is the author of *Pan Dulce*, a book of poems. He teaches English at Incarnate Word High School.

LORI MARIE CARLSON-HIJUELOS is an editor, translator, and novelist. She lives in New York City.

WILLIAM SLOANE COFFIN served as chaplain of Yale University and Williams College and was senior minister of Riverside Church and president of SANE/FREEZE: Campaign for Global Security. He became famous while at Yale in the 1960s for his opposition to the Vietnam War, was jailed as a civil rights "Freedom Rider," and was indicted by the government in the Benjamin Spock conspiracy trial. He was immortalized as Rev. Sloan in the *Doonesbury* comic strip. He died in 2006.

PAT CONROY was the bestselling author of many books including *The Water Is Wide*, *The Great Santini*, *Beach Music*, and *The Prince of Tides*. He died in 2016.

MARIO CUOMO was the fifty-second governor of New York and served three terms from 1983 to 1994. He died in 2015.

TIMOTHY EGAN is a journalist and op-ed columnist for the *New York Times*. He has written several books, among them *A Pilgrimage to Eternity*, *The Immortal Irishman*, and *The Good Rain*, which won the Pacific Northwest Booksellers Association Award in 1991.

ALAN EHRENHALT is a journalist and nonfiction author. A graduate of the Columbia University Graduate School of Journalism, he has published several books, including *The Lost City: The Forgotten Virtues of Community in America*, *The Great Inversion and the Future of the American City*, and *The United States of Ambition: Politicians, Power, and the Pursuit of Office*.

SHADI FEDDIN is a young professional who has worked in the financial industry as well as the start-up sector in New York City. Originally from Omaha, Nebraska, she enjoys being a citizen of the world and travels often.

RALPH FLETCHER is the author of picture books, nonfiction, and novels for young readers. Among the books he has written about the process of writing are *A Writer's Notebook*, *Poetry Matters*, *Live Writing*, and *How Writers Work*.

VALERIE GRIBBEN, MD, is an assistant professor of pediatrics at the University of California, San Francisco (UCSF). Her writing has been published in the *New York Times*, the *Wall Street Journal*, and the *Los Angeles Times*.

She is the author of the young adult novel *The Fairytale Trilogy*. Website: valeriegribben.com.

ALEXANDRE HOLLAN was born in 1933 in Budapest and has lived in France since 1956, sharing his time between Paris in winter and the south of France during summer. He paints exploring the limits of perception, trees in summer, still lifes in winter. His notes on painting and drawing accompany his research. Some have been published by Eres: *Je suis ce que je vois: Notes et réflections sur la peinture et le dessin, 1975–2020*. His work is represented in Paris and Brussels by the gallery La Forest Divonne, and in the south of France by Galerie Mirabilia in Lagorce.

MOLLY IVINS was an American newspaper columnist, author, political commentator, and humorist. Born in California and raised in Texas, she attended Smith College and the Columbia University Graduate School of Journalism. She died in 2007.

GEETA KOTHARI is the nonfiction editor of the *Kenyon Review* and director of the Writing Center at the University of Pittsburgh. Her writing has appeared in various anthologies and journals, including *New England Review*, *Massachusetts Review*, and others. She is the author of the short story collection *I Brake for Moose and Other Stories*.

JEREMY LEE is a chef and restaurateur who lives in London, England.

YUYI LI is a young professional who loves to create art and enjoy cultural experiences. She grew up in Chengdu, Singapore, and North Carolina. Yuyi now lives and works in New York City.

EMILY LISKER is a writer, painter, and musician living in Woonsocket, Rhode Island. She loves to read poetry, swim with her dog, Romeo, and bake sourdough breads.

KAMAAL MAJEED is a communicator who shares his wisdom about humanity, race, and self-realization through his words and his teaching. He continues to empower those whom he meets on the path to becoming.

MADGE MCKEITHEN writes essays and teaches nonfiction writing in the undergraduate writing program at the New School in New York City. She is the author of *Blue Peninsula: Essential Words for a Life of Loss and Change*. Her essays have been published in the *New York Times Book Review, TriQuarterly, Utne Reader, Lost and Found: Stories from New York, Lumina,* and *Best American Essays 2011*.

NAWAL NASRALLAH, a native of Iraq and an award-winning researcher and food writer, specializes in Middle

Eastern cuisine, with a specific interest in Iraqi food and culture and its history. She is the author of *Iraqi Cuisine: Delights from the Garden of Eden*, and translator into English of two medieval Arabic cookbooks from Iraq and Egypt.

SCOTT PITONIAK is a nationally recognized sports columnist and bestselling author of more than twenty-five books. A native of Rome, New York, Scott has been a journalist for nearly a half century and has taught journalism at St. John Fisher College for thirteen years. He resides in Penfield, New York, with his wife, Beth, and has two grown children and two granddaughters.

ANNA QUINDLEN is a journalist, opinion columnist, and novelist. Her *New York Times* column, Public and Private, won the Pulitzer Prize in Commentary in 1992. Among her many novels are *One True Thing*, *Black and Blue*, and *Still Life with Bread Crumbs*.

MICHAEL J. SANDEL is the Anne T. and Robert M. Bass Professor of Government at Harvard University and the author of the *New York Times* bestseller *Justice: What's the Right Thing to Do?* His work has been the subject of television series on PBS and the BBC.

RAQUEL VALLE SENTÍES is a poet, playwright, and artist who was born and raised in Laredo, Texas. She started writing after taking a creative writing class at Laredo Junior College in 1988. Her poetry has been published in many anthologies, and her first collection, *Soy Como Soy y Qué*, published in 1996, won the international Premio de Literatura José Fuentes Mares in Letras Chicanas, awarded by the Universidad Autónoma de Ciudad Juárez, Chihuahua, México.

DAVID E. SKAGGS is a former six-term Democratic member of the United States House of Representatives from Colorado's 2nd Congressional District (1987–99). Skaggs currently holds positions as chair of the board of the US House of Representatives' Office of Congressional Ethics and vice-chair of the board of trustees of the National Endowment for Democracy. He was the founding co-chairman with then Congressman Ray LaHood (R-Illinois) of the House bipartisan retreats, designed to improve bipartisan relations among House members. He has remained dedicated to improving the quality of the nation's politics.

GARY SOTO, poet and essayist and finalist for the National Book Award, is the author of many books, including *Living Up the Street*, *A Summer Life*, *Buried Onions*, and *New and Selected Poems*. He is the author of "Oranges," one of the most anthologized poems in contemporary literature. He lives in Berkeley, California.

ALEXANDRA STODDARD is a philosopher of contemporary living and the bestselling author of twenty-eight books, including *Living a Beautiful Life*, *You Are Your Choices*, *Things I Want My Daughters to Know*, and *Choosing Happiness*.

KELLYNOEL WALDORF is a scholar, a writer, a feminist, and a graduate student who is also a teacher at North Carolina State University in the field of linguistics.

GEORGE WASHINGTON, a native of Virginia, held various posts during his lifetime as a farmer, military leader, and statesman. He became the first president of the United States in 1789.

YING YING YU is the daughter of immigrants. As a teenager, she began articulating, through writing and speaking, the essential life lessons steeped in tradition that her family has shared with her. She continues her journey today on the way to becoming.

Copyrights

Excerpt from "Notes of a Translator's Son" by Joseph Bruchac. Reprinted from *I Tell You Now: Autobiographical Essays by Native American Writers*, edited by Brian Swann and Arnold Krupat by permission of the University of Nebraska Press. Copyright © 1987 by the University of Nebraska Press.

"Cool Beef" used by permission of Jeremy Lee. Copyright © 2001 by Jeremy Lee.

Excerpt XVI from "If You Are What You Eat, Then What Am I?" Used by permission of Geeta Kothari. Copyright © 1999 by Geeta Kothari.

Excerpt from "Homemade Mayonnaise" from *The Pat Conroy Cookbook: Recipes of My Life* by Pat Conroy, copyright © 2004 by Pat Conroy. Used by permission of Nan A. Talese, an imprint of the Knopf Doubleday

Acknowledgments

I would like to thank my incredible family; my spirited agent, Jennifer Lyons; and my faithful editor Caitlyn Dlouhy, who, with the help of her first-rate team at Caitlyn Dlouhy Books, helped me bring this book to light.

About the Editor

Lori Marie Carlson-Hijuelos was born in Jamestown, New York. She earned her master of arts in Hispanic literature at Indiana University and has taught at several universities, including most recently Duke University. Carlson-Hijuelos has edited and written numerous books for children, young adults, and adults including the groundbreaking *Cool Salsa* and *Red Hot Salsa*. *The Sunday Tertulia* was her first novel and was a Barnes and Noble Discover Pick. She lives in New York City and currently devotes most of her time to the literary estate of Oscar Hijuelos. You can reach her at lorimariecarlson.com.